Debt Free
or
Die Trying

FIRST EDITION

By Marcus Garrett

Creator of
DebtFreeOrDieTrying.com

Contributor
PaychecksAndBalances.com

Disclaimer

The information contained within this book is strictly for educational purposes. If you wish to apply ideas contained in this book, you are taking full responsibility for your actions.

The author has made every effort to ensure the accuracy of the information within this book was correct at time of publication. The author does not assume and hereby disclaims any liability to any party for any loss, damage, or disruption caused by errors or omissions, whether such errors or omissions result from accident, negligence, or any other cause.

This information is provided and sold with the knowledge that the publisher and author do not offer any legal or other professional advice. In the case of a need for any such expertise consult with the appropriate professional. This book does not contain all information available on the subject. This book has not been created to be specific to any individual's or organizations' situation or needs. Every effort has been made to make this book as accurate as possible. However, there may be typographical and or content errors. Therefore, this book should serve only as a general guide and not as the ultimate source of subject information. The author and publisher shall have no liability or responsibility to any person or entity regarding any loss or damage incurred, or alleged to have incurred, directly or indirectly, by the information contained in this book.

Foreword

I'll be honest with you. If, after reading the title of this book, your first thought was of all the reasons you won't be able to succeed, then this book might not be for you. My goal is not to convince you I'm the guru of debt-free living.

Getting out of debt is not easy. It is very difficult. Sometimes it feels impossible. You probably already know this, which is why you're reading this book. I won't pretend that my story is the best or easiest example of how to get out of debt. It's likely that my life is not the best example, and the journey I took is definitely not the easiest route to debt freedom.

What I can tell you is that I was once buried in over $30,000 in debt. I lived check-to-check and often paid credit cards off with other credit cards. Life sucked. I sucked at life. Unfortunately for me but lucky for you, this sucky life experience allowed me to develop a very particular set of skills that were acquired over a long life of financial irresponsibility. If the lifestyle I've described sounds like how you're living now, have lived in the past or want to avoid living in the future this book will help you or that friend you know that is living the lifestyle of the fast and the financially frivolous.

Before we get into what this book is, we should first talk about what this book is not. This book isn't meant to talk *at* you. It's meant to talk *to* you. I take pride in managing expectations. "Under-promise and over-deliver." I find managing expectations makes people's lives, including my own, easier. I like to know what people expect of me, and I like to know what I can expect of people. For the sake of this book, I'll assume you're the same way. I also like to assume a lot.

This book is not a tirade against credit cards, loans, private or nonprofit companies or credit in general. Used responsibly, credit is and will continue to be a very useful and necessary tool in most of our lives. Unfortunately, some people use credit irresponsibly or never learn to use credit responsibly. My hope is that this book can be one of many small steps you'll take to prevent yourself from being one of those people who spend their lives using credit irresponsibly, because as one of those people, I can confidently say it's not fun being that person.

Lastly, in full disclosure, I believe you should know about some portions of my lifestyle so you can determine how they compare, relate or conflict with your own. I only offer this information so you can honestly assess how relative and applicable my experience, and lessons learned, might be to your life before moving forward. I like to believe the advice I'll recommend is relevant to everyone, but to manage my expectations and yours, please keep the following in mind:

- **Single**—When I wrote this book, I was unmarried. For the majority, but not all, of my debt-freedom journey I was single. At various times, I was in a committed relationship with women who in roughly equal parts helped decrease and increase my debt. I cover this in some areas of the book, where applicable, but this book is not focused on how others helped or harmed my goals of living debt free. I do believe you can get out of debt while in a relationship or marriage, but it will take a far more concerted effort to get two people aligned with what is admittedly an already very difficult pursuit for even just one person to accomplish. With this in mind, if you choose to pursue a debt-free lifestyle, I highly recommend that you share and preferably ensure your partner has this same goal in mind, and they are willing to make the sacrifices necessary for you both to succeed. Clearly communicating your goal will make both of your lives much easier, because as I'll elaborate on in the body of this book, there will be sacrifices one or both of you will need to make that will impact both of your lives. Being debt free is a noble goal, but retrenching on promises or a lifestyle your partner has grown accustomed to without communicating how your choices will impact them is not something I am recommending. In my life, it was faster to pay off my debts alone, but it was also more rewarding when I had someone to share the victory with.

- **No Children**—I recognize children add an additional variable, and potential lifestyle expense, that I can neither comment on nor directly relate to beyond my experience dating women with children of their own. Once again, I believe the general ideas covered in this book are sound whether or not you have children, and if I am significantly incorrect in this reasoning, I guess I will just have to write a second book when I have kids.

- **Investments**—Because this book focused on my debt-freedom journey, I won't cover much in the way of investments. I have had and continue to have various investments, none of which bias my opinions on tips and strategies for debt management. I make no recommendations on the "best or worse" options for choosing how to allocate your debts and investments or choosing whom to invest with or use for help managing your debt. In these areas, I simply recommend you choose the apps, software, or investment/debt management strategies best suited for your specific goals.

- **Public transportation**—I figure this area is minor but worth mentioning. I just want to point out that my transportation expenses were greatly minimized. I owned a car, but I paid it off in 2010. I cover how I accomplished this later in the book. However, this achievement was immensely helped by the fact that I rode public transportation to and from work each day for an extensive period of time while paying off my debt. For this reason, beyond car loan payments, the majority of this book will not cover expenses related to transportation (cost, repairs, etc.), as this particular expense category has been minimal to negligible for me.

Dedication

I would like to dedicate this book to everyone who has tried, failed and still refused to give up. This book is for you.

In the realm of financial support, I must thank all of my past and present employers who allowed me to be gainfully employed since the age of 16 (I assume some of you regret employing me, but I thank you for not firing me despite the regret you might feel in hindsight). Without your meager-to-generous donations to the patent pending "Keep Marcus Employed Foundation," I would not have managed to be a tax-paying citizen who climbed out of debt and who occasionally had the discretionary income to enjoy dessert wine and usually keep my light bill paid on time.

I also want to thank all the people in my life, far too many to name individually, for their help and support over the years as I pursued my goal of debt freedom. Specifically, I would like to take the time to thank my mother and father, family and friends. Without your love, support, mentorship and willingness (sometimes forced) to listen to my complaints throughout this journey I know I would have never succeeded. Many of you provided emotional and mental support, and in some cases, financial assistance. Your help has not and will never be forgotten. You mean the world to me. I cannot thank you enough, but I am truly indebted to all of you and thank you generously from the bottom of my heart.

Table of Contents

Introduction

I know this introduction is slightly longer than 140 characters, so I hope you can find it in your heart to read the next few sentences. However, I completely understand if you need to take small breaks to catch up on social media and whatever else in your life is more important than reading the current sentence you are currently reading in that voice in your head in which you read sentences. If you want to know more about me, the author of this book, as well as my personal journey in and out of debt, then the entirety of the book is for you. You see, this book took me a lot longer to write than I thought it would take to write when I agreed to write it back when I was a recovering blogger. Blogs took minutes to write. This book took years. I blame only myself, because apparently I have the attention span of Dory—the lovable character from the Nemo movies. I say all this to say, if you don't bother to read the entirety of this book and we should ever happen to meet in real life or communicate on social media? Please lie to me! Tell me you read every word if for no other reason than to cater to my already delicate sensibilities and unjustifiably inflated ego. Thank you.

Please enjoy.

Debt Free or Die Trying
Part 1: Burying Myself in Debt

In America, and perhaps everywhere, getting into debt is surprisingly easy. If you're reading this book, you probably already know this fact of life. It's not just easy, it's comically easy. You're only one credit-card-fueled night out, badly planned investment, extended hospital stay, misplaced co-sign or loan-funded college educational pursuit from thousands of dollars of debt. If you're a baller, this is no big deal. If you're a non-baller, like myself, a few thousand dollars in debt is a very big deal. It can derail your entire life. In my case, my battle with debt derailed my life for almost a decade.

Like most financially irresponsible people of my generation, I got my first credit card when I was 18 years old. I didn't know anything about credit cards. At that time I didn't know much about money management, either. Basically, like many 18-year-olds, I thought I knew a lot; I was wrong. My naivety combined with my arrogance made me the perfect target demographic for debt accumulation. I was young and dumb yet legally old enough to make contractually obligated purchases that were consistent, impulsive and irresponsible. I doubt a credit card company could have fantasized about a better customer than the 18-year old version of myself.

In fact, the companies represented on my college campus during freshmen orientation thought I was the perfect candidate for a credit card. I might as well have had a target

2

DEBT FREE OR DIE TRYING

painted on my chest. I had a job, but I didn't make a lot of money. Logically, I didn't have a lot of disposable income. Illogically, the representatives of these fine financial institutions thought I warranted ownership of multiple credit cards. I had somewhere in the neighborhood of five to 10 credit cards before I was legally old enough to drink, which, I guess, is a good thing because in subsequent years I would pay for a lot of liquor with those same credit cards.

I remember walking through my dorm's community area when a guy asked me if I wanted to sign up for a credit card and get a free T-shirt. The line was filled with equally ignorant people my age, so logically I assumed if everyone else was doing it, I should be signing up as well. We were sheep being led to financial slaughter. I wonder how my other free T-shirt-clad peers have fared in the debt department.

After all, I'm sure we all owned a debit card. In my mind, this made me a financial expert. My basic understanding of credit cards, not exactly corrected by the guy helping me fill out the paperwork, was that banks gave you free money and all you had to do was pay them a minimal amount of that money back each month. In my 18-year-old mind, it all seemed pretty straightforward.

As I was filling out the paperwork for my first card, the guy helpfully explained that a number of areas weren't that important and that I didn't need to bother filling them out. In most scenarios, skipping over large portions of a contract I never bothered to read might trigger alarm bells. I was 18, though. I didn't have time to be bothered by pesky details or fine print on a contract I never bothered to read when there were free T-shirts and logo-embossed Frisbees to choose from. I picked out a T-shirt emblazoned with the logo of a company I'm fairly certain has since filed for bankruptcy, as well as a yo-yo, Frisbee and pen and then went on about my day, promptly forgetting about the whole incident until a few weeks later.

I didn't know at the time, but years of experience have taught me that credit cards show up like something mailed to you from the National Security Agency. It's all very top secret. I appreciate the credit card's thinly veiled attempts to hide my credit card from would-be thieves, which I assume is to ensure that only I can cause contractually irreparable harm to my financial well-being. It's not like anyone with foul intentions would ever open an anonymous envelope emblazoned with the words 'do not open' anyway.

Having forgotten the original ordeal of becoming a credit card holder, I had no clue what might reside inside that first credit card envelope. In hindsight, that ominously vague envelope would contain the worst thing—financially speaking—to ever happen to me at that point in my life. It was an all-black credit card. This is not to be confused with a Black Card, which is only given to people who can afford things I can only fantasize about buying while waiting in line to buy lottery tickets.

In my ignorance, I didn't realize the impact of being awarded my first credit card. I also grossly underestimated the impact it would have on my life. Once again, I ignored the contract that accompanied the card. I called the number on the attached sticker to activate it, placed it in my wallet and moved on with whatever remedial activity 18-year-old men engaged in during the early 2000s, probably rhythmic shuffling to the soulful sounds of "Whoomp There It Is."

It was weeks, or possibly months, later before I used my credit card. I can't remember the first purchase, but I like to imagine it was for something reasonable, like food, water or 22-inch rims. As with many people now burdened with thousands of dollars of debt, I started simple enough. I'd buy something I wanted here or there. Often, I was perfectly capable of paying cash for these items. I assured myself that I'd pay off the credit card in full as soon as the bill arrived. However, whenever I saw the awe-inspiring low cost of the "minimum payment," I couldn't possibly justify paying more. "What am I, an idiot? Let the banks take all the risk!" I imagine my 18-year-old self might have said to himself as I convinced myself that next time would be the actual time I paid it off in full.

Surprisingly, the first few years I owned a credit card I didn't make any substantial purchases, never buying much over a few dollars. It's amazing how even minor purchases, coupled with astronomical APR rates, can add up over the years. Soon, all those one-off purchases from month to month added up to hundreds of dollars. Eventually, it was thousands of dollars. Still, it seemed like no matter how high my outstanding balance grew, my minimum payment always remained low. This low monthly payment was quite the mathematical feat in my young mind. I believe I even thought I was winning and the banks were losing in this game of financial chess.

Over time, I started getting more and more credit card offers, which of course I was all too eager to complete. What mere mortal could resist those "zero percent APR," "zero percent balance transfer" slogans? Before long, I had three or four major credit cards on top of the two or three my college credit card pals had signed me up for on my first day of school. I read somewhere – probably on the Internet – that you shouldn't cancel credit cards, so as a financially savvy up-and-coming expert of the world, I would open new credit card accounts anytime a better offer arrived in the mail. For all the irresponsibleness of my irresponsibility, I'm proud to say that I only missed one credit card payment in my entire life. But, that's jumping ahead in the story.

In fact, the first couple of years went pretty smoothly. From 18 to 20, I only racked up a few thousand dollars in debt. Humble beginnings! You might even say I was the one who truly, "started from the bottom." I didn't really start hitting the big-time debt misfortunes until I became roommates with an old high school friend. Don't get me wrong, it wasn't his fault. He always paid his half of the rent on time, a compliment I can't make for latter-year roommates. I do, however, attribute some blame to my apartment complex, which introduced me to the customer-friendly opportunity to make rent payments via credit card. In the race to capitalize on the financially ignorant, our apartment managers were light years ahead of their time.

In fairness, I can't speak to how other apartment managers worked. For me, accepting credit cards for rent payment was the rough equivalent of Saint Peter asking me if I want to cut in line at the gates of Heaven. Technically, I was living on my own. Until this point, I had spent the entirety of my freshmen year living in an on-campus dormitory where I could depend on stable housing and a relatively stable meal plan—a meal plan I often prematurely spent one quarter of the way through each semester gorging on midnight snacks and assorted goodies. If you're failing to notice the pattern here, I was compulsively irresponsible when it came to managing money.

Nevertheless, I thought the idea that my apartment managers would accept credit cards was nothing short of an earthly blessing from the almighty Himself. I had some vague recollection of how to be responsible from the youthful renaissance period before I owned credit cards, when cash was my only option. I knew, in theory, I was supposed to maintain some semblance of a budget, and my multiple credit cards were supposed to be used for cases of "emergency." However, what defines an emergency at age 20 versus age 30 is subjectively as wide as the expanse of the universe. As I signed my apartment's 12-month contract with my roommate, rent-on-credit sounded perfectly practical. Reality, on the other hand, unfolded a little differently. In the beginning, paying my rent with my credit card was the exception, rather than the rule. The "beginning" is defined here as a short period of time that unfortunately is nowhere as encompassing and close to "towards the end."

Soon, I found it increasingly difficult to justify paying rent with my hard-earned cash when my easily earned credit cards were sitting idle in my wallet. As with most addictions, denial was my first high. Every month I charged a hit of rent to my credit card, I assured myself that that time would be the last time or, my personal favorite despite not having any additional disposable income to support this fantasy, I told myself that I would "pay myself back" the following month. After I got tired of lying to myself, I just completely gave up on the idea of paying off my credit cards each month. In a stroke of "genius," I assured myself I was going to college, so that when I graduated and I was a big baller I could totally pay off all my debt in like a "couple months." I justified my flawed logic with quotes you might see on thrift store T-shirts, or the bumper sticker of cars released in the 80s but adorned with rims and accessories from the 21st century. You Only Live Once! and other similar cliché quotes convinced the younger me that once I graduated from college I would be Balling Out of Control, and would be able to pay back these nominal expenditures in The Blink of an Eye because It Is What It Is. With the pesky restrictions of responsibility completely shed, I finally allowed myself to freely Make it Rain, on credit.

One might be surprised to know that I did have a job at this time. My job was to complete catalog orders in a call center for approximately $9 an hour, but I'm sure I had a grandiose title worthy of my financial expenditures like *Telephone Payment Compilation Scientist*, or something to that effect. Not that it mattered because I pretty much used my credit cards to pay for anything I didn't feel like paying cash for, which was nothing. To make matters better (or worse), I'd also apply the same logic to my friends' expenses.

If mis amigos didn't have a means to pay, I used my credit cards to fill the gap between the lifestyle I should have been living and the lifestyle we wanted to live. Naturally, this extended to any woman, or women (usually women), I dated formally or informally. Demonstrating my eclectic appreciation for the finer things in life, I decided to put a loud bass system in my car as well. Also, no used car of mine would be complete without equally tasteful waist-high chrome rims to accentuate my overpriced, credit-funded sound system. Fortunately, this was only the beginning of my plunge into drowning in debt. One such trip that moderately captures the opulent spending of my youth comes to mind.

The NBA All-Star weekend came to Atlanta my sophomore year of college. My friends and I decided we *had* to go. To do anything less, like study for the midterms we all had coming up that week, made so little sense to us that going on an impromptu road trip didn't even warrant a debate. We *had* to go to the NBA All-Star weekend. Since we went to different schools, we made plans to meet in Austin, Texas, before making the 13-hour road trip to Atlanta, Georgia. We were too young to rent a car, but one of our older friends agreed to sign over the rental car as long as we promised to be responsible. She clearly overestimated our capacity to meet this promise, but nevertheless her misplaced trust was our gain.

The week of the trip, I realized I only had $20 cash on hand, which given my income management skills at the time, was a pretty good week. A wiser man, or even someone who wasn't a complete idiot, might have decided to abstain from the trip when realizing his weekend budget was limited to a maximum of three McDonald's happy meals. Young me lacked such forethought and wisdom. I simply decided that anything beyond $20 would go on any one of my many credit cards, which I had somehow managed not to max out, yet.

DEBT FREE OR DIE TRYING

My inability, but not lack of will, to max out my cards probably had to do with the fact that each month more credit card offers arrived to notify me that my credit limit had been increased or they had a better offer with lower interest—and more credit. Coincidentally, my credit limits always seemed to increase right when I needed to buy or do something I had no business buying or doing. It's as if the credit card companies had an algorithm synchronized with my financial ignorance. Our trip to Atlanta was no exception. By this age, I had at least $10,000-$15,000 in available credit extended to me.

Between my three friends and me, we were lucky if we had $53 in total cash. On the bright side, one of our friends had family in Atlanta, so we really only needed gas money – plus food and water, if you want to split hairs. We set out on the 13-hour drive, promptly driving in the wrong direction for four of those hours, before self-correcting on the newly estimated 16-hour, one-day trip. The rest, as they say, is history.

I can't lie. It was a great trip! For legal and moral purposes, I can't cover all the details in this particular book, and it's not as if I remember 80% of the events anyway. Even if I did, I would deny it. What I do know is that I left Austin with approximately $2,000 in credit card debt, and I returned to Austin with about $3,000 in credit card debt. You might balk at the idea that I mysteriously spent $1,000 in credit and $20 in cash in a single weekend, but I assure you that 20-something me felt this was money (and credit) well spent.

DEBT FREE OR DIE TRYING

This credit card spending binge was but one of many examples of my inability to care about how much money I spent, as long as the money I spent was on my credit credits and not with my cash. I never thought about how much debt I was accumulating in those early years. It seemed like no matter what I bought, the minimum payments were always manageable. If the minimum payments were manageable, 20-something me assumed everything was fine. This flawed mindset would haunt me for many, many years. My ability to outright ignore my growing debt was so easy that I literally never thought about it. I chose to ignore this obvious problem, and for a long time, it was simple to do so.

Why?

Most of my debt was accumulated in small purchases. Apparently, I preferred to kill my credit with a thousand debits rather than the more obvious wound inflicted by one gargantuan purchase. Save for the occasional credit-financed road trip, I guess I was somehow self-conscious enough not to make large purchases. There was one very large and very expensive exception to this experience.

> Before the perils of texting while driving were made available among your local TV commercials, I was a chronic text-driver. During one particularly passionate text-driving incident I took my eyes off the road for what seemed like only a brief moment. Granted, given that I was texting using a 10-key Nokia bar phone, it was probably closer to 15 minutes.

> Before my eyes returned to the road, I was suddenly careening into the median. However, I wouldn't exactly describe what transpired as a "wreck." That

would be giving too much credit to the ignorance of the situation. No, I was able to self-correct before I did any major damage to mine or any other vehicle. What I did manage to do was flatten both of my tires on the driver's side. My car nearly disabled, I willed it to a side street before running completely out of options.

I had two choices now.

There was the logical first choice: I could call my parents, who had access to AAA, and explain the situation. I'd likely receive a lecture and possibly have my car taken away.

Then, there was the illogical second choice: I could call my friend who had no AAA and no money but who would provide moral and logistical support, and, while he may laugh at my plight, he would not lecture or take my car away. Please note that this incident predated social media, so his smart remarks would be limited to my face versus Myspace or Facebook. In later years, the possibility of being made fun of in person *and* social media may have weighed heavily on my final decision. But, naturally, using the same cell phone that had gotten me into this predicament, I called my friend.

Before he arrived, I managed to get a spare on one of the tires. I now had 50% less of a dumbass, self-inflicted problem: one flat tire. A generously empathetic person might call this progress. The only thing more nonsensical than what you'll justify spending money on in your 20s is what you won't spend money on. My financial decision-making in this situation was very telling.

DEBT FREE OR DIE TRYING

Despite spending thousands of dollars on mundane material objects for myself and others that had no appreciable value—many of which I had lost, given away, or no longer possessed—I balked at the suggestion of my friend to call a tow truck because that was, as I described it to him, "[expletive] expensive." I was convinced I could drive my impaired vehicle to a local repair shop that I used because I had convinced myself that my repeat business there meant they ripped me off slightly less than the many closer repair shops I could have opted to go to.

My friend, loyalty unquestioned, agreed to follow me the 10 or so miles it would take to get to the repair shop with his hazard lights on to prevent me from being rear ended, while simultaneously sacrificing his own vehicle for said rear ending, as I drove somewhere between a slug and a snail's pace to prevent my flattened tire from coming completely off the rim before I arrived. A few hours into what should have been a 10-minute drive, we made it to the repair shop. That's where the real fun began.

After a brief diagnosis, the repair shop informed me that they estimated the damages to the vehicle were somewhere in the thousands—they couldn't say for sure because they had no idea how much labor it would take to un-mangle my currently mangled axel and rims. The tone of his voice was a measure of disbelief and confusion. He; in all his years as a mechanic mange had never seen the result of something so dim-witted. I like to imagine my repair remains one of the top urban legends he regales his mechanic friends with over drinks when they talk about the "craziest repairs they ever saw."

Once again, I was faced with two choices. I could call my parents, who might or might not (but likely not) help me with the costly repairs, take my car away and/or give me a lecture, or I could charge the whole thing to my multiple, near-maxed out credit cards, regardless of cost, and take this story with me to my grave (or now, until my parents read this book). To the surprise of no one, least of all you the reader, I chose the second option.

I told the mechanic to proceed with the repairs, which, in retrospect, probably cost more than the value of the used car and perhaps even a brand new used car, combined. Twenty-four hours, a few thousand dollars (with an equal amount of tears shed) and two credit cards charged later, I had my car back.

"Good as new!" – 20-something year old me.

It was official. I finally realized I was in DEBT. I swore off credit cards! But, I hadn't even made it into the credit card elite league yet, which I define as those with greater than ten thousand dollars in debt. I only thought I had problems. Amazingly, I would be responsible for quite some time before forgetting everything I had learned. Besides, my minimum payments were far too manageable for me to remain responsible forever.

Spring semester of my sophomore year of college, I randomly decided I had enough of the University of Texas-Austin. It was only when I was older that I realized I had misattributed my poor grades and near failure at school to the rigors of university life, rather than my lack of commitment to university life. With the clarity of wisdom, I've now accepted that I was remarkably lazy, never studied and especially didn't like doing anything that might resemble working hard in school or in life. While the full backstory to why I transferred might be more or less interesting to some readers, the decision itself was more reflective of my own impulsive-decisions-character-flaw than my unsustainable debts, which were merely engorged by the same yet unrelated impulsive-decision-character-flaw. Therefore, specific to my justifications for leaving college? I won't bore you with the details.

****

My parents put up surprisingly little protest to the idea that I was going to transfer schools as long as I met two qualifiers: 1) it didn't cost them any additional money; and 2) I didn't drop out of school – an eventuality I believe they had secretly accepted was inevitable based on my GPA and general inability to maintain a full course load for a complete semester before deciding it was "too much to handle" a few weeks into each semester. If that's what they believed, I don't blame them. I offered no reason not to come to that conclusion. However, in reality, I never planned to drop out of school. I *hated* school, but I also couldn't think of anything better to do with my spare time or how I would make any money without a college education. After all, I had credit card bills to pay.

In defense of my youthful ignorance, I did manage to hold down steady jobs while going to college. For the most part,

DEBT FREE OR DIE TRYING

I even showed up to the majority of my classes, as long as I found them interesting and they started after 9:00am. I just didn't prepare very much before I got there, try very hard once I arrived, or study after I left. Besides these minor limitations, I was a model student.

So, in the summer of 2003 at the ripe old age of 21, I randomly picked another public university to attend. If I had specific conditions beyond ensuring it was a public college that was covered by the program my parents used to help pay for my school—I was great at managing everyone else's money but my own—I don't remember them. But rigorous analysis and extensive preplanning doesn't sound like something the younger me would have burdened himself with. In the end, I chose Sam Houston State University over a few options in Houston. Honestly, I was scared the city of Houston was too close to my family and friends. I at least had the foresight to accept that I didn't have the mental discipline necessary to attend college in the same zip code as my similarly aged, equally irresponsible peers. I was perfectly capable of reckless negligence on my own. I didn't need additional assistance. With some minimal transfer paperwork and a summer break, I was officially SHSU bound.

For reasons that remain unclear to me even to this day, I was convinced that once I graduated college, I was going to get a job balling so hard and so out of control that it wouldn't matter how much debt I had accrued. I turned out to be mistaken, and looking back, I have no idea why I thought getting a college education would entitle me to large sums of annual income in the first place. I'm aware that there is a relative correlation between college education and income, but I can assure you it's not nearly as strong as the relationship I had made up in my head. I thought if you didn't know how to rap or weren't athletically gifted—two areas where I, unfortunately, failed to excel—then college was the next best "get rich quick" scheme. As a result, during college, I was never particularly concerned about how much debt I was accumulating nor did I ever make a concerted effort to start paying off my credit cards.

This is where things got weird (or weirder). Have you ever watched a poorly scripted movie with a hard-to-follow storyline? It's as if one second things make perfect sense and the next second you're completely lost? That movie you have in your head right now pretty much covers what happened with me and my debt load during my junior and senior years of college. One year, I was merely a few thousand dollars in debt from moderately, yet reasonably, irresponsible endeavors. Then the movie that is my life cuts to another scene—approximately 12 months pass—and suddenly I was tens of thousands of dollars in debt.

I wish I could impress you with a story of woe and suffering about how I was forced into over $10,000 of debt in just under two years. But, honestly? I don't remember how it happened. It's as if I went to sleep with some semblance of responsibility and woke up indebted. I can't recall all of the individual ignorant activities, but there is at least one repeat scenario that still haunts my subconscious (and wallet).

Spring Break(s): South Padre Island, Texas—For those of you who are not from Texas, I will still assume you are loosely familiar with the concept of 'Spring Break,' even if you didn't attend college or for that matter, don't live in America. However, just in case you are not versed in this college experience, Spring Break is an American-themed holiday, which I believe originates from farmer times when kids had to return home to help their families till the land. While the majority of Americans no longer till farm land, for whatever reason Spring Break continues to exist.

Spring Break, as I remember it, was basically a seven-day exodus that allowed my friends and me to reunite and cram our already impressively reckless activities into 168 hours of continuous reckless activities and unchecked moral debauchery. Since I didn't have much cash at the time—because if you haven't been paying attention, I paid for everything on credit, lived check-to-check and was generally careless with any leftover amount of money I might have been able to save—I put almost all of my Spring Break excursions and related expenses on my credit cards. In principle, this meant approximately each year I bulk-spent several thousand dollars on hotels, rental cars, alcohol and other miscellaneous, yet equally dumb, activities because I felt it was my personal responsibility, and mine alone, to ensure my friends, my friends' friends and I all had the best seven-day Spring Break vacations of all time.

Don't get me wrong, folks. I love Spring Break! Most college kids, including myself, only attended college for the official (and unofficial) breaks, not limited to spring. Everything may have a price, but the price limit for ignorance is infinite.

DEBT FREE OR DIE TRYING

In a lot of ways, I only know Spring Break took place because there are plenty of photos documenting my physical presence, even if I was clearly mentally absent. That said, there is no debating the fact that these trips—and others like them—cost me several thousand dollars. Unfortunately, all I have to show for them are blurred memories. There are no assets. No investments. There will be no return on the amount of alcohol and other mostly legal activities I engaged in with my friends in the future except for perhaps a failed liver or early onset Alzheimer's. I don't regret the decisions I made in my past. I simply regret how much they negatively impacted my future. But, maybe that's how life works.

Seriously, I truly wish I could accurately enumerate all the ways I managed to increase my debt load over 600 percent in less than three years if not to benefit myself, at least you the readers. Trust that I have tried. In some ways this budget-amnesia I have represents the impact of not having a budget, or even remotely knowing how much money you spend or owe, can have on your lifestyle. It's hard, perhaps even impossible, to address a problem you don't even recognize exists. For a long time I was able to make all of my minimum credit card payments, so I assumed things were fine. Out of nowhere—at least in my head—I began having trouble just making the minimum payments on three to four of the six to seven credit cards I had opened. Eventually, the financial situation became so bad that by my senior year of college I began postdating checks (something I later found out had zero impact on when they were cashed) and mailing checks I didn't have money in my checking account to cover. I merely hoped they wouldn't arrive at the credit card company before my direct deposit. Other times, I would open new credit cards just for the "low introductory rates" and transfer payments from one credit card to buy myself a "free" month of not making a credit card payment.

I was slowly becoming a professional debt shuffler. Instead of "robbing Peter to pay Paul," I somehow managed to rob myself while paying someone else at double the interest rate. I convinced myself that as long as I paid the minimum amount each month for each credit card balance, by any means necessary, then I was ahead of the game. In reality, I was burying myself deeper and deeper in debt and putting off the eventual reckoning. Perhaps the only thing more troubling than the false reality I had created for myself was the fact that I somehow never had trouble obtaining credit from any number of interested lenders. From age 18 to 22, I was never turned down for a credit card. In fact, in my entire life, I've only been turned down for one credit card. I later found out that was due to a fraudulent charge on my credit report. Still, believe me when I tell you that if you ever get to a point in your life when you're paying off credit cards with other credit cards, you are not winning at anything, let alone the game of life.

Through a miracle, God, luck or all of the above, I was able to keep my debt shuffling sham going until I finished college. I graduated in 2005 with a strong C, a degree in Business Administration and a little less than $10,000 in personal debt. A college diploma owner now, I figured the hardest part was behind me. All I had to do was show this priceless piece of paper to a few employers and surely they would pay me more than handsomely. In my mind, the obvious next steps were to get rich, pay off my debt at my leisure, get married, have kids and maybe even buy a small dog and a two-story, 2,000-plus square foot home with a white picket fence in the suburbs. Just like in the movies!

I was gravely mistaken. The worst part of what would become a decade-long struggle with debt hadn't even begun. Until I stepped out into the post-college world, I only thought I had problems. Post-college life had other plans for me.

Debt Free or Die Trying
Part 2: Rock Bottom

"The first step to getting yourself out of a hole is to stop digging." – Ancient Common Sense Proverb

At age 22, despite thinking a bachelor's degree entitled me to riches, employers didn't seem to agree with this grandiose personal assessment. My first job out of college started at about $19,000, and I was happy to make that amount. It took over three months just to get a call back for that job. Although I was happy to be employed, my ego was devastated when I realized I had just spent the last four years of my life earning a degree so I could make less than $9.00/an hour or about $2.00/an hour more than I was making before the degree. This was my "American Dream"?

While I was grateful for any work by that point in my job search, this wasn't exactly the "dream job" I had in mind when I sat in my dorm room staring at the ceiling imagining a lifestyle of "making it rain," P. Diddy White Parties and Playboy Mansion weekend vacations during sabbaticals from my coastal summer homes in the Hamptons and Florida Keys. In addition, because I had saddled myself with almost $10,000 in debt, I barely made enough money to cover my monthly minimum credit card payments. For this reason, I moved back in with my parents shortly after graduation. Other than college breaks, I hadn't lived at home full-time in almost five years. I can't speak for my parents. But for me, the situation was less than ideal. I was miserable.

DEBT FREE OR DIE TRYING

As I struggled to fix my life, I became increasingly depressed. I thought there must be a mistake of some kind. Why wasn't I balling out of control? Why was I living at home? In the impassioned pleas of Jerry Maguire, why wasn't anyone ready to "show me the money"?

This didn't make any sense! Someone had made a terrible mistake. They just needed to correct it. You would think during this time that I would have learned to live within my means, make a plan and focus on getting out of debt as soon as possible so I could move forward with my life. I admire your optimism. You, however, would be mistaken.

Like any logical person, I wanted to get out of debt. In fact, I had concocted the best-laid plans during those first few months out of college: I'd live at home for a few years—a plan I can neither confirm nor deny I shared with my parents—while paying off all of my debts before moving out into the "real world" debt free.

It was the perfect plan, but as it has a habit of doing, real life intervened in my fantasy. First, my parents and I drove each other completely insane. In hindsight, I'm not sure who was to blame. Like Mark Twain, the older I get the more I am astonished by how much my parents have learned. If only they had been this wise when I was young and immature. For example, they had the ridiculous idea of wanting me to pay rent to live in their home. The audacity of charging me to live in a home, lest I need to remind you dear readers, a home I had lived in rent free for 18 years of my life.

In my mind, this was like charging prisoners rent to stay in jail. I didn't even want to live at home, so why would I pay rent to be there? I should clarify here and now that it would be years later before my father confided that after witnessing my budgetary habits firsthand, or lack thereof, my mother and he mutually decided it would be to the benefit of everyone if they managed my money for me by charging "rent" and placing the funds in an interest-bearing account for when (or if) I moved out. As with most things, my parents had my best interest at heart. Of course I assumed they had the worst in mind because, as rapper slash actor Willard Christopher Smith, Jr confirmed for America in 1988, "All across the land, parents just don't understand."

Perhaps coincidentally, I also met a girl—whom, naturally, I assumed would be my wife now that I had a college degree—immediately after graduation. I was 23, so of course I assumed this made me a "grown ass man". I had also recently received a promotion at work to a new position balling out of control for about $30,000 a year. I wasn't going to let a little thing like years of wisdom and parental advice stop me from making a fool of myself. So, despite my parents' best efforts, I moved out of their house approximately three months after moving in. I got an apartment in town that was only slightly more accommodating than living on the streets and encompassed the approximate square footage of a large moving box.

Less than one month after obtaining my marginally better than a box with a roof excuse for an apartment, I asked (or she forced, I can't honestly recall) my then-19 year old girlfriend of a few months to move across the country to live with me. She had no degree and no gainful means of employment. But, she was FINE—meaning very beautiful for those readers who are not bilingual children of the millennial slang. Her physical attractiveness made her more than sufficiently qualified to move in given my 23-year-old minimum standard relationship requirements.

Since my lovely significant other didn't have a job or supply any measurable means of income to the household—something I hadn't considered before she moved in—paying the bills fell on my shoulders. I guess this wouldn't have been so bad in itself if we weren't both high maintenance, heavy spenders. This may come as a surprise to some of you, but after taxes $30,000 doesn't stretch very far. Because cutting back on our unnecessary expenses would have made too much sense, I began looking for ways to make more money to cover living outside of our means. I paid for our extreme budgeting by doing what I did best: charging everything I could get my hands on to credit and hoping that God or someone equally sympathetic to my plight would rescue me one day. During this time I had the bright idea of signing up for one of the many consolidation loans I had received in the mail pretty much every week. With the clarity of hindsight, I can confidently say that this was easily one of the single dumbest financial maneuvers I would make in my entire life.

I don't have anything against consolidation loans. Used correctly, as it turns out, they can be useful tools for helping responsible people manage their money and get back on a path of debt management and eventual debt freedom. At age 23, I was neither responsible nor seriously looking to be debt free. I had an arbitrary goal of achieving debt freedom by 28. Still, since I had no plan on how to achieve this goal, doing so was about as useful as saying I wanted to own a unicorn by age 28 considering the feasibility of achieving either goal would have been exactly the same.

DEBT FREE OR DIE TRYING

Having never signed up for a consolidation loan, I assumed—because it would make sense—the loan company would pay off my outstanding credit cards and I would begin making one loan payment each month for the next 60 months. In a world filled with reasonable people and common sense, this imagined scenario is likely the course of action that would have taken place. Unfortunately, we do not live in such a world.

Instead, once approved, I received a check in the mail for $10,000. Mailing someone who is coming to you to assist them in their budget-management, because they have demonstrated for nearly a decade that they do not know how to budget or manage was the equivalent of mailing me a blank check or a winning lottery ticket, since either scenario would have resulted in the same irresponsible outcome.

Well, I wasn't completely irresponsible with the consolidation loan. I applied half the check to two of three outstanding credit cards. But wholly unreasonably, in a mind-blowing act of stupidity that I can only reflect on with a mix of horror and pity, I used the other half of the check to go on a shopping spree for my girlfriend and myself because "we earned it." I have no idea what "it" was we earned, but I do know we spent a lot of money because of it.

Possibly proving that Einstein's theory of infinite ignorance is true, I used the remaining few thousand dollars to put a down payment on a used car. In summary, in a mad dash of blind ignorance, I doubled my debt burden—barely even paying off the original debt I'd accrued—from almost $10,000 in credit cards to $10,000 in a consolidated loan, a

DEBT FREE OR DIE TRYING

few thousand dollars left on the original credit card I didn't pay off with said consolidation loan, and now I had a car loan for over $13,000. This was so impressively ignorant that I feel the need to illustrate it for you in two tables.

Table 1: Rock Bottom:

Debt Before Debt Consolidation

Debt	Amount
Credit Card #1	$4,000
Credit Card #2	$2,000
Credit Card #3	$3,000
Total Debt	**$9,000**

DEBT FREE OR DIE TRYING

Table 2: Rock Bottom:

48 Hours after "Debt Consolidation"

Debt	Amount
Credit Card #1	$0
Credit Card #2	$0
Credit Card #3	$3,000
Consolidation Loan	$10,000
Car Loan	$13,000
Total Debt	**$26,000**

In one weekend, I nearly tripled my debt and added a 60-month car loan to my portfolio of ignorance. If irresponsibility were a skillset, I would have been a rocket scientist, rather than the idiot I actually was. I didn't know it then, but I would spend the greater part of the next eight years paying off debt I accumulated in less than eight hours. Irresponsibility is a funny thing. You would think the weight of crushing debt would have been enough to stop me from spending so recklessly, and maybe, if I lived alone, it have would been.

DEBT FREE OR DIE TRYING

But, with a new financial enabler in my life, I had to keep up false impressions. So, on an income of $19,000 with $26,000 in debt, I decided the best thing to do was move into a more expensive apartment.

To be fair, this decision wasn't solely my girlfriends' fault. At any time, I could have pointed out that neither she nor I could afford the lifestyle we were attempting to live. In an act of misinformed chivalry, I felt it was my direct responsibility to make sure the bills were paid, even if many of those bills were self-imposed and outside of our means. Therefore, when she told me she wanted to move to a nicer, yet more expensive apartment across town, I only put up minimal protest. I liked nice things, too!

Besides, we weren't moving into a five-star hotel. It's just that when you're broke, every dollar counts, and we weren't even counting or budgeting the very few dollars we had. By now, she did have a job working at a local bank. Yet, increasing your expenses more than your income every time you get a raise does not a budget make. That would also assume we had a budget in place to break, which we did not. We lived check-to-check, and when our checks ran out, we lived from credit card to credit card.

Since no immature couple is complete without buying crap they don't need, we also set out to buy some furniture for the apartment we couldn't afford, along with a new flat screen HD TV we also couldn't afford. For a mere $3,000, I was able to get a "great deal" on the latter purchase by opening up an allegedly low-interest loan. Despite making low-money, we were living the high-life.

DEBT FREE OR DIE TRYING

We had a new apartment, and every time we had a little extra money, we bought new toys. I wasn't even pretending to manage or pay off my debt by now. I was just happy to make minimum payments. With the consolidated loan, I was able to recreate the impression of having more money than I really did since I owed several different parties several thousands of dollars. The falsely low monthly payment made me feel like we had more money each month. Perception was reality. When we weren't busy buying new things we didn't need, we went to clubs in town or in other cities to waste even more money we didn't have. I was broke, but I'd be lying if I said I wasn't having a great time living life. But like all good parties it had to come to an end.

DEBT FREE OR DIE TRYING

Table 3: This is What "Rock Bottom" Looks Like

Debt	Amount
Credit Card #1	$0
Credit Card #2	$0
Credit Card #3	$3,000
Consolidation Loan	$10,000
Car Loan	$13,000
Flat Screen TV Loan	$3,000
Total Debt	**$29,000**

With dreams of grandeur in her 20-something mind, my girlfriend decided that small-town living wasn't going to cut it for the lifestyle she (or we?) needed to live. I wanted to keep her happy, and fortunately, my job did have offices located in Austin, Texas. I had grown up in Austin, so like most people's fondness towards their hometowns, I had solemnly sworn never to return.

DEBT FREE OR DIE TRYING

Austin isn't a bad city, but like any city where you spend most of your life growing up, you're bound to make some friends and some enemies. I didn't have a long list of enemies, but I was still no less eager to return to the city where I had spent ten years of my youth making them. Since the prime Austin nightlife area is condensed to one long block decorated with bars known as "Sixth Street," I knew I was bound to run into my fair share of ex-girlfriends, ex-guy-friends and ex-friend-friends. I was doing fine spending and living outside of my means without involving the support of my frienemies, whom if I saw I would obviously have to 'stunt' for to prove how much better than them I was doing in life. In spite of these red flags, I requested a job transfer. It was approved. I notified the apartment manager at the complex where we lived that I would be breaking the lease to move back home—another bill. I wasn't thrilled about the process, but at least I had my girlfriend. Well, I thought so anyway.

On the contrary, while I was making tentative plans for our future, my girlfriend was making more specifically defined plans for her own future. A part-time model when I met her, something I was admittedly well aware of, she received an offer to model in New York City. I might have been able to compete with a lot of things, but New York City was not one of them. The decision seemed pretty straightforward. She was going to New York. It was really only a matter of if I did or did not want to join her. For all my cumulative years of ignorance, the idea of traveling across the country with no job and no prospects did not strike me as very appealing when every month I had bills due that I could barely afford even under the most ideal circumstances. I loved her, but even emotional immaturity wasn't enough to supersede one obvious fact: I *needed* a steady paycheck.

DEBT FREE OR DIE TRYING

Even if I did want to go with her—and a part of me did—there was no way in hell I could survive more than 30 consecutive days without a constant, and now progressively higher, paycheck. I had accumulated far too much debt by that point. Also, when considering the fact that she had recently lost her job at the bank before this new opportunity arose, if I didn't pay our bills, who would?

I don't want to oversimplify the decision behind this process, because it was very difficult. Yet, simple math dictated that I needed to work, consistently and often. I wasn't going to stop her from going to New York, but there was no way I could go with her. Since I had already received the transfer at my job, I was going to have to move to Austin by myself and find a new apartment. Fortunately, since I did have some friends back home, I linked up with an old high school friend. I told him that I would need a roommate. I drove to Austin by myself one weekend, and he and I were able to find a reasonably priced place.

We signed the paperwork, and I drove back home to tell my girlfriend the news. As quickly and as chaotically as we had begun, we were ending. She began traveling to New York more and more frequently before making her final move. During that time, I began planning my transition to Austin. By the time she left for good, I, nearing 25 now, was stuck back in Austin. All I had to show for my troubles and debts since college was a used car and a big screen TV. In some ways, being heartbroken by this particular experience probably kept me from spending more money. For a long time, all I did was work, pay bills, come home, and repeat. I was too tired to date, and I was too depressed to go out. I was emotionally drained, but budget-wise this was one of the most responsible periods of my early 20s.

****

Austin was about three times as expensive as where I lived before. Because I did most things on impulse rather than intelligence in my early 20s, I didn't factor the cost of living impact on my meager income before the move. Soon, I had to find a second (and sometimes third) job just to cover my bills. In addition to working full-time, I would pick up odd contract jobs in the evenings, weekends or nights. I did everything from building computers, selling phones for commission and working nights and weekends at hotels. Basically, if I wasn't asleep, I was working. If I wasn't working, I was asleep. This was one of the very few times in my life when I wasn't increasing my debt, but only because I didn't have time to do so.

During one of my many random odd job searches, I found a similar job to my own with a respectable pay increase. Unfortunately, I was only minimally qualified for the position. I applied, but I didn't expect much to come from it. Even as I was going through my second- and third-round interviews, I half-expected to be turned down. To be clear, I liked my current job. I had only been working there about 12 months but that didn't change the fact that I needed more money, period. It was a good job, but there wasn't a raise or opportunity for promotion in the foreseeable future. When the new job called with a firm offer, I jumped at the opportunity. This was the first time in at least three years when I began seriously thinking about getting out of debt.

DEBT FREE OR DIE TRYING

With my new raise, I thought this was as good a time as any to look at a new consolidation loan. I figured with the lessons learned from my first experience, I could negotiate a reasonable rate and make a financial change for the better. I was half-right.

I did make a positive change, but when I called a large, reputable institution for a consolidation loan of $15,000 in response to a pre-approved offer they sent me in the mail, I received another life-altering reality check. By the time it was over, my mindset about money would be changed forever.

By 2008, I had over $30,000 in debt from various credit cards, personal loans, an outstanding school loan and accumulated interest. I hadn't realized how close to the fringes I was living until missing one credit card payment was a haunting eye-opening experience. It was actually one of the first credit cards I ever opened. Somehow, I missed the bill in the mail. Without warning or much sympathy, my next credit card bill had an APR of 29.99%. This was more than a 300% increase from what I was used to paying. With all my other bills barreling down on me, I couldn't even afford to make the minimum payment. Given the loyal customer I had been for the past half-decade, I figured a simple phone call would correct the issue. I called customer service and explained that I had never missed a payment. I was also happy to pay the minimum amount and associated fees for both months but that there was no way I could continue paying at an APR of 29.99% on the thousands of dollars I had on the card. Their response?

"That's not our problem."

DEBT FREE OR DIE TRYING

I made what I now know is a very dumb, emotionally-based decision. I didn't want do business with them anymore. To teach them a lesson, I self-sabotaged myself by making several poor financial decisions:

> First, I demanded they close the credit card immediately. That will teach them, a multi-billion dollar empire, I thought. In reality, I was hurting myself far more than I was hurting them given that your credit card score is calculated based, in part, on how much available credit you have—a fact I didn't even know at the time nor did they volunteer.

> Second, using a balance transfer option from another card that already had a ridiculously high balance of its own, I transferred the debt to another credit card. This was an equally misinformed decision because of the standard balance transfer fee, which, although part of a low-interest deal, was likely equal to or higher than the 29.99% interest I would have ended up paying on the original card. It seems I preferred the avalanche method of poor-decision making to the slower snowball effect.

> Lastly, because I didn't know how and had never budgeted a day in my life, when the next month arrived, I was as surprised as anyone to find out that it would be impossible for me to just make all the total minimum payments. It was five years since I graduated college, but financially, I was in the exact same infantile position as when I left—once again, I was unable to make minimum payments on my credit card debt.

DEBT FREE OR DIE TRYING

I had received several consolidation loan offers over the years since my last epic fail. Paranoia and fear kept me from taking them, but now I didn't have a choice. If I didn't do something, soon I wasn't going to be able to pay any of my bills. Possibly as soon as the next month. Was I really going to be one of those case studies of young millennials filing for bankruptcy in their 20s?

Panicked, I began looking through the most recent offers for one with the lowest APR. A well-known, large institution stuck out from the group. For some reason, I trusted this offer. Maybe I figured that if a large bank who specializes in making loans for a living was giving me a preapproved offer, then surely I must be responsible. Otherwise, what would warrant them taking such a risk on me? Why would a bank extend credit to someone who couldn't manage it? That consolidation loan offer gave me a sense of self-validation. That pre-approved loan made me feel like I was important and people liked me. I figured my situation couldn't be that dire if banks were still offering me even more credit. I just had to get this loan, make some positive budgetary changes, and then everything would be OK.

Denial is a powerful drug.

With nothing but hope to guide me, I called the phone number on the front of the consolidation loan. I had no plan. Actually, I had no idea what I would do if they turned me down. Failure was not an option. Subconsciously, I might have known that if this conversation didn't end well, I would be looking at a downward spiral that would likely only terminate through bankruptcy. I did my best to push those thoughts out of my mind so I could sound make-believe friendly and confident when the loan consolidator answered my call. I really just wanted to cry and beg the loan company to extend me an offer. By that point, I literally would have taken anything they gave me. After several years of juggling my debts in a mirage of fiscal responsibility, my back was against the wall. I had to get this loan. My options were dwindling. Sooner than later, I would be option-less.

I'll never forget this conversation, because it would forever alter the trajectory I was on. I now understand that the loan person was just doing his job. I'm sure I was one of hundreds, if not thousands, of people he spoke with. He had every right. I was down on my luck and we both knew it. But, it was still hard to listen to the arrogance in his voice as he spoke down to me on the call. I was placed on hold several times while he entered my information. He'd come back, ask a few questions, type and then place me on hold again. I assume behind the scenes they were processing were calculating whether I would be accepted and for what amount, if any. More accurately, he was literally calculating my future. I could only hope in silence that he got the numbers right.

As I waited in silence with nothing but my thoughts to haunt me, it dawned on me that the loan company had several options at their disposal. I had none. They could approve me instantly, place my offer in a queue for further consideration or outright deny me. I was playing a game of Financial Roulette, but only they had the power to pull the trigger.

There have been few times in my life when I've felt less in control. I was peppered with questions. He

38

hesitated with each of my responses as if I'd answered none of them correctly. I was nervous and became increasingly agitated with the process. If they were going to turn me down, just tell me so I could begin wallowing in self-pity and self-medication. My frustration seemed only to amuse the operator more, or maybe I was drowning in my own emotion. After minutes that seemed like hours, he came back with an offer.

Both the monthly payment and interest rate was higher than the "pre-approved" offer I had in my hands. In fact, based on the many APRs I'd seen over the years, the rate just seemed high, no matter how you looked at it. I informed the operator as such. Undaunted, he told me "based on his calculations" their company's offer was more than fair because, on average, the interest rate was lower than many of my current credits cards. For example, "The one you just closed had an interest rate of 29.99%," he reminded me.

He also pointed out that my monthly payments, in total, were higher than the monthly payments they were offering—a fact that I had, ignorantly, forgotten to even calculate, so I had to assume he was telling the truth. I didn't have my bills in front of me to confirm or deny his assertions. Even if I did, I hadn't made a budget in 25 years of my life, and I certainly wasn't going to develop one in the next 25 seconds.

If this was a chess match, he was five moves ahead of me. Disgusted, I realized I could have continued disputing but it would have only been in an effort to put off the inevitable. I knew—and possibly so did he—I was going to have to take whatever they offered me that night. I'd rarely felt so disgusted with myself. Acknowledging defeat, "I'll take the offer."

"We'll get that right out to you," he said, and with that he hung up the phone in my face.

I should have been overjoyed. I had an $18,000 loan on the way that would finally allow me to consolidate all my outstanding credit into one "low" monthly payment. If I stayed disciplined, I would make my final payment by age 30. Instead, that night was one of the lowest points of my life. How did I let it come to this? How had I let my debts grow to a point where I couldn't even pay the *minimum* monthly payments despite the fact that I was constantly working anywhere between one and three jobs a month?

I was tired. I was sick. I was sick of being tired. I made a vow to never let my debts get that bad again. I hadn't acknowledged it until then, even though it was painfully obvious. I had a problem. I had reached rock bottom.

If you believe in such things, this is where being a stubborn, ISTJ, Scorpio—all personality descriptors that might be redundant statements—finally helped me start on a legitimate path to debt freedom. My stubbornness made me determined to get myself out of debt. My pride made me never want to allow someone to have that much control over my life. I *never* wanted to feel this hopeless again. Through my own doing, I had put my fate in someone else's hands. I hated coming to that realization. For the first time since I opened a credit card at 18, I was unwavering in my resolve to get out of debt.

DEBT FREE OR DIE TRYING

The only problem was I only had a goal. I still didn't have a plan. On the bright side, at least I was finally serious about managing my debt. Even though I was properly motivated, it would still take a few more years for me to figure out what the sacrifice of budgeting and debt management would truly mean.

Debt Free or Die Trying
Part 3: Getting out of Debt
(Finally)

Making the decision to get out of debt was one of the easiest things I have ever done. Actually *sticking* to the decision to get out of debt was one of the hardest things I have ever done.

It turns out, spending money and living outside of your means for years is a lot easier than developing a budget and sticking to a plan for half a decade. Not only is debt management not fun, generally and specifically speaking, in my case, it also takes *a lot* longer to pay off debt than it does to accumulate debt. It would take me about three times as long to get completely out of debt as it did to get into debt.

I blindly tripped, stumbled, failed, pushed and sometimes outright stopped while on my journey to debt freedom. This time, though, I always started back more determined than ever. Usually, motivated by remembering that debt consolidation loan phone call I had made at age 25.

"Never again," I'd repeat to myself.

During the first part of seriously pursuing debt freedom, like most haphazard decisions I am prone to make, I simply had a goal: I wanted to be debt free. This was a goal. I often confused it with having a plan.

DEBT FREE OR DIE TRYING

A goal without a plan is about as useful as dreams to an insomniac. Nevertheless, at least I was motivated, even if I didn't exactly have a clear path to success. It turns out that even misguided direction is sometimes better than no direction at all.

While I had been working several odd jobs over the years, I finally accepted that working one job simply wasn't going to bring in enough income for me to meet my goal of being debt free. Instead of working contract jobs on a freelance basis, I began applying for part-time jobs I could do on the weekends in addition to my full-time job. I put my pride aside and accepted that maybe, despite my college degree, I wasn't going to get rich working one 9 to 5. Lottery winnings notwithstanding, I needed the combination of two (or possibly three) incomes if I wanted to pay off my debts in my lifetime.

I'm sure there were a lot of options I could have chosen. I chose a part-time sales job with a major phone carrier because they were the first employer to call back. Luckily, the company also paid a decent hourly wage, plus commission. Had I been more responsible, I might have completely paid off my debts in a few years by simply allocating all of my part-time paychecks toward my debts. However, despite all that I had been through, responsibly spending and budgeting was still far too foreign a concept for me to adopt immediately. I took the more mature but slightly less advisable route of allocating the majority of my part-time job's paychecks to my debts, but not all of it. If you must know, the rest of my money went to miscellaneous adventures, none of which were as legendary as those college Spring Break trips.

DEBT FREE OR DIE TRYING

I was maturing, but I was by no means mature, yet. Even when you have the "scared straight" moment in your life, old habits still die hard. I used my new extra cash to revisit old habits. I hadn't been able to go out much since all of my full-time income was eaten up by just paying my debt. I took this opportunity to start going clubbing, again. I took several vacations, and basically lived the most fiscally irresponsible life I could possibly imagine during my rare off-work hours. My only redeeming quality, which I'm sad to admit, is that at least I didn't use my credit cards to fund these adventures in ignorance this time. So, while I was still being ignorant and immature with my money, at least I was no longer funding these extravaganzas on credit. Between bottle popping, random trips and occasional dabbles in relationships of varying seriousness, I did manage to pay down some of my debt.

Despite these moderately noble accomplishments, there was an x-factor I forgot to take into consideration when I began working 50 to 80 hours a week: I was getting older. When I was in my early 20s, working 80 hours a week and sleeping four to six hours a night would have barely registered as an issue. As my early 20s gave way to my late 20s, exerting myself for 24 -to-48-hour periods without sleep had a detrimental impact on my ability to function. My age, coupled with the excessive partying and drinking during what few off hours I had, begun to take its toll on me and my performance at the full-time day job. Eventually, I had to choose, and I realized I didn't have the energy or the willpower to continue working two or more jobs for the rest of my life, even if it was helping me manage my debt.

DEBT FREE OR DIE TRYING

Confronting this sad realization, I quit my second job so I could focus on my main job. This decision meant I quickly went back to living check-to-check. Fortunately, the small dent in my debt I had made with the part-time jobs allowed me to live slightly above my means on one paycheck. But, besides whatever IRS refund I might receive at the beginning of the year, I still had no savings set aside, so I was always one paycheck away from spiraling back into crippling debt. Having a non-existent savings meant I was constantly subject to the real possibility of burning through my credit cards if I ever lost my job or if anything went remotely wrong in my completely random, already hectic life.

Unless something changed, I also realized that I might need to live with a roommate—as I did at the time—for the rest of my life. Despite the life-changing revelations of my mid-20s, I was no closer to owning a home, buying a car or doing much of anything that would demonstrate I was progressing towards making the transition from being a menace to society—or a personal menace to myself—to a fully functional, positively contributing adult member of society.

Due to the many poor decisions I had made in my past, I was either going to have to work two jobs again or look for another job if I wanted to make any significant progress in my life. With these debts hanging over my head, I felt like I wasn't ready to pursue a serious relationship. A part of me didn't want to burden anyone else with my financial problems, which were self-created in the first place. Furthermore, I was in some ways scared by the way I managed my money the last time I committed to a woman. I figured there was no way I could manage myself, money *and* a relationship at the same time.

DEBT FREE OR DIE TRYING

Looking back, this mindset was unfair to the women I dated. I extrapolated my poor money management experience with one woman to represent how I and any woman I dated might manage our money. This narrow-minded thinking made me assume a successful relationship could only occur *after* I learned successful money management skills on my own. In other words, I convinced myself I had to get out of debt *before* I could make other positive changes in my life, including being in a serious relationship. Managing my debt became my sole focus—most times at the sacrifice of all my other life goals. To assist with meeting this goal, I began looking for a job that might help. Opening myself to possibilities across the country, I began looking for work that offered a higher income.

As with most of my well-intentioned, half-assed ideas, I thought my search for work would take years given the fact that I began looking for jobs at the beginning of what would later become known as the country's second worst recession. Yet, as was my luck with most poorly thought-out plans in my life, I received a call from a job offer in Denver, Colorado less than four weeks later. After a successful interview, I was made an offer the same day. It came with a significant pay increase, I think.

Actually, to this day, since I didn't account for a cost-of-living adjustment, I continue to wonder if everyone simply broke even in that salary negotiation. Assuming you could call a "negotiation" me asking for a number I thought sounded cool that I think I heard in a movie once and them agreeing almost immediately to it. I toss in my bed thinking about this some nights but in the theme of this book, I've had no choice but to, "charge it to the game."

DEBT FREE OR DIE TRYING

To spice up the jeopardy of the unplanned move to a City where nobody knew my name, the job also came with a six-month mandatory probation. Meaning I could be fired, without cause or explanation any time during the six-month period. I guess no good deed goes unpunished. The probation, the move, and the half-planned action itself gave me what I believe people smarter than myself refer to as a "conundrum."

Because it wasn't a well-thought out plan, I had several things to consider: I had a girlfriend at the time that I would have to leave behind. I would be moving to a state where I had never lived to work in an office I had never seen. The six-month probation meant I would be leaving a state that I had called home for 27 years to possibly be laid off 180 days later in the middle of The Great Recession. To put it lightly, it was an intimidating decision to make. But I had just under $30,000 in debt and no known way to pay it down. Therefore, this decision wasn't really a decision. It was an ultimatum. It was a chance I had to take in the present, whether I wanted to or not, because of the many mistakes I had made in the past.

All I had was hope and faith that this decision would be the right one to propel me towards one day reaching my goal of being debt free, so I put in a two-week notice with my job in Austin. I sold everything I owned that wouldn't fit into a used Toyota Camry. Less than six weeks and one 13-hour road trip later, I had moved to Colorado. Fortunately, this experience would become a blessing in disguise.

Debt Free or Die Trying
Part 4: Good Luck

I've heard, "Luck is when preparation meets opportunity." I've been very lucky. It would take another three years, but using the methods I describe below, I finally paid off all my debts. By age 30, I was completely debt-free.

When I was mired in debt in my 20s, I thought being completely debt free would be a claim I would never make. It seemed hopeless. I realize now that at any age, any type of debt sucks. Sometimes debt is a necessary evil. Sometimes it's inevitable. Other times, debt is self-imposed accidentally or with purpose. One of the main reasons I wrote this book is to inspire others to see that they can get out of debt (or ideally, why they should avoid getting into debt in the first place).

While this book isn't meant to be an instruction manual, below are a few other final pieces of advice to keep in mind as you begin, transverse or end your journey to debt freedom.

Good luck!

Debt Free or Die Trying: The Three Principles

DFDT Principle #1: 75% of the battle is mental.

The most difficult part about getting out of debt was stopping my self-sabotaging. Before I finally accepted how bad the problem was I had already managed to get myself into tens of thousands of dollars of debt. Worse still, other than a used car, I had no single appreciable asset to show for it. Don't get me wrong. I had a great time funding my life with credit cards. Hell, even a few of my friends have great stories and great times to reflect on because of my reckless spending, and what was my reward?

After college, I wasn't even 23 years young and already had more than $26,000 in debt – and I wasn't even done! It would be another two years, and thousands of dollars later, before I finally made the decision to get out of debt. The only thing crazier than how long it took me to choose to stop living outside of my means is that no one was ever going to stop me. Living outside of your means is as American as apple pie. The "American Dream" is literally built with debt. Besides those friends that read this book, I doubt anyone knew or cared how I managed to buy so much despite making so little.

The decision to stop living beyond my means was my responsibility. Taking responsibility for your spending habits will be one of the most difficult and most important decisions you make before pursuing a successful debt freedom plan. Until you are serious about getting out of debt by any means necessary, you will fail. Don't waste your valuable time. Once you accept that reality, you're more than halfway there, because that first step is one step most people never take. As I said in the beginning, 75 percent of the battle is mental. Make the choice to be debt free no matter what it takes, then embrace your decision and do whatever it takes to be debt free.

DFDT Principle #2: Debt freedom does not look cool.

Being debt free is cool. Becoming debt free is not cool.

There is absolutely nothing cool-looking about getting out of debt. You will have to make sacrifices. Lots of them! For example—and I know this is the equivalent of asking you to volunteer to drown to death—you might even have to give up the following non-exhaustive list on a temporary basis: name brand everything, cable, the latest smart phone, new music, etc.

I don't want to traumatize you, but the list goes on and on. I gave up all of these things for a few years along the way. I wasn't complimented on my clothing or expensive dates for a long time because I wasn't doing either one of them. I was called cheap more often than I can name, though I obviously prefer the term "frugal," but you know what? Who cares! That's was it took to be debt free and it is what it is.

I'll put it in simple terms: If you're spending money on anything non-essential to your survival, then give it up. You're wasting money on instant gratification when that same money could be used to get you completely out of debt, forever. That's a lifetime of gratification. To make sure there is no confusion, I'm defining "non-essential" as anything that doesn't contribute to your ability to maintain access to food, water and shelter. The top three expenses for American households are housing, transportation, and food.

In addition to taking on an overwhelming amount of debt, when I finally developed a budget I also realized I had taken on significant lifestyle creep. With every increase in pay I engaged in lifestyle inflation. In effect, every "increase in pay" I got was eaten up by an equal or more extravagant increases in crap to buy. My ratio of crap-to-buy to pay increases was not balanced. Once I realized this, I made some simple changes that had a significant impact on actually putting money back in my pocket. Another non-exhaustive example:

Table 4: Lifestyle Deflation

Expense	Approximate Monthly Savings	Annual Savings
Rent (roommate)	$300	$3,600
Food (eating out less)	$100	$1,200
Cable (canceled)	$200	$2,400
Miscellaneous	Various	$1,000*
Total		**$8,400**

Asterisks (*): For years, I gave up new cell phone and electronic purchases, name brand clothes, and yes, haircuts ($20 a week x 4 a month = $960/year). I also cut back on discretionary spending on stuff like movies, coffee from a chain that shall not be named, etc.

Before I made a plan to get out of debt I never had a budget. My budget planning consisted of spending until I ran out of money and then figuring out how I was going to make it to my next paycheck. I was surprised how little changes each month could save me thousands of dollars a year. In addition to the mental exercise of actually tracking my money, which helped me better manage my money, short-term sacrifices led to amazing long-term gains. In the table above, for example, the simple act of not having cable for five years meant I saved myself $12,000 ($2,400 annual savings x 5 years) on an expense I chose to have, and then I made the decision not to have in my life. It's not that I don't like cable, I do. I just prioritized paying off debt over watching the latest TV dramas.

While on a true debt freedom plan, you may not be the coolest dressed person in the room, party, club or lounge. However, you can take comfort in knowing that you will likely be one of, if not the only one, in the room that is financially responsible. Years from now when many of those same 'cool-looking' people who were always dressed in the latest fashions and owned all the newest gadgets are drowning in the exact same type of debt you paid off five or ten years earlier, you can celebrate in the present while they struggle through the decisions of their past. Resist the incessant need for instant gratification. You deserve better.

DFDT Principle #3: *Failure is always an option.*

Unless you're perfect, you will fail while you are on your debt free plan. Expect it. Embrace it. Then, get over it. For the sake of this book, failure *is* an option.

Failure builds character and makes the taste of victory, which you will achieve, even sweeter. It sounds cliché but the beauty of getting out of debt is that you will succeed simply by never giving up. You didn't get into debt overnight. You won't achieve debt freedom overnight. If you set up a sound and reasonable plan, which I hope this book has helped you do, then debt freedom is literally inevitable.

If getting out of debt was easy, everyone would do it. The easiest route to a debt free life is to avoid getting into debt in the first place. Since you're reading this book, I'll assume you didn't follow that plan. That's OK. The first step is recognizing you have a problem. Congratulations! Now, let's take the next step. Let's fix the problem.

Debt Free or Die Trying:
The Four Keys to Success

DFDT Key #1: Define the problem.

One lesson that took me far too long to learn was to define the totality of my debt. I also should have developed a budget much sooner than I did. I recommend you do this in the beginning of your journey rather than midway or the end, as I did. If you have a lot of debt, determining "how much" isn't as easy as some might think. For one, you might not know or readily have access to the total volume of debt you have. For this reason, I recommend you begin by requesting your credit report. By federal law, you are entitled to at least one free credit report from all three major credit bureaus each year. You can read more information about the law and access your report through the Federal Trade Commission's website at https://www.ftc.gov.

I, on the other hand, charged everything. Rental car? Charged it! Vacations across the country? Charged it! Good time? Charged it! It didn't matter what the expense, I assumed (incorrectly) that I'd eventually be able to pay it off. I have no idea why. I had no plan beyond lofty aspirations fueled on the fumes of hope.

In my semi-defense, credit card companies kept offering me credit. If you have good credit, there will always be a lender around the corner eager to enable your irresponsible habits.

DEBT FREE OR DIE TRYING

This is also sometimes the case if you have bad credit. Quick life hack I learned the hard way so you don't have to:

Please.

Stop.

Being.

Irresponsible.

Now.

Just because someone offers you credit does not mean you know how to responsibly manage credit. For example, despite never making more than $9/hour my entire college career, by the time I graduated I had somehow amassed well over $30,000 in available credit lines. This meant I had the ability to spend $30,000, plus interest, before I secured my first job out of college making a whopping $19,000 a year. In some ways, given all my financially frivolous adventures, it is amazing I didn't max out all my credit cards in my teens before coming to my senses in my twenties.

When I was younger—and don't ask me why I thought this way—I figured that banks were knowledgeable, billion-dollar institutions that would never extend more credit to me (or anyone) than I (or they) could afford to pay back. I believed in that fantasy for the five years I attended college at two four-year institutions—neither of which provided me with something as simple as an education in financial management. The real world taught me Personal Finance Management 101 using some of the hardest tests I never wanted to take. It was a painful lesson that I don't want to repeat and that I strongly recommend you avoid.

DFDT Key #2: Set a reasonable goal.

Originally, I wanted to be debt free by age 28. It was arbitrary. It was a simple goal I set out to attain because it sounded good. I did not succeed. I didn't succeed because I never calculated how much I would need to actually pay to be debt-free in five years. I simply said I wanted to be debt free and I assumed I would will my way to success. Do. Not. Think. Like. Me. I was wrong. To succeed, you need to set a (reasonable) goal first, then make a plan to meet that goal.

After college, I worked two or more jobs until I was in my mid-20s, and I still wasn't making enough money. Had I actually had a budget and a strict timeline, I would have known this long before I turned 28 and realized I still had $20,000 in debt left to pay off.

It's great to have a timeline, but if it's unreasonable, it's pointless. Unreasonable timelines only set you up for frustration and failure. Setting a timeline forces you to evaluate whether your current income, salary, and budget will even allow you to succeed. The no-plan plan is a favorable plan because it requires no plan, no measure of success or failure, and in most cases, no action. You're also unwittingly planning to fail. Setting a debt free goal with no timeline is not setting you up for success sooner than later, it's only setting you up to procrastinate on paying off your debt never than sooner. If you want a plan that will actually succeed, you need to set a timeline and a budget at the beginning rather than the end.

DEBT FREE OR DIE TRYING

DFDT Key #3: Implement your plan.

Now that you've got a plan, implement it and be patient. You will not get out of debt overnight. Depending on the amount of your debt, it will take a long time, years even, because it will usually take you longer to get out of debt than it did to get into debt. The sooner you accept this fact the easier the already difficult journey will be.

On a related note, I'm not a fan of getting out of debt with a group of friends. If you are going to use a 'groupthink' strategy for tackling your debt, I recommend you use strangers before friends or family. You might be asking, "Why?"

There is an "I" in credit. In many cases, debt is accumulated on an individual basis (school loans, personal loans, credit cards, etc.). Therefore, sometimes getting out of debt might be easier to tackle on your own, rather than with a team. I know that's counterintuitive, but you'll need to strike a balance between finding support and overcoming another unnecessary obstacle. For instance, have you ever been on a diet with a group of friends or a loved one? When, or if, they fall off the diet, isn't it more difficult for you to stay disciplined?

Debt is the same way. If you or someone else in the group falls off first, it'll make it harder for you to stay focused and disciplined when you and the group are no longer on the same plan. Getting out of debt is already hard enough. You want to minimize any opportunity to 'fall off' and maximize opportunities to 'stay on'. Debt management can be, but doesn't have to be, a team sport.

DEBT FREE OR DIE TRYING

If you're not careful, others' failures will give you an excuse to fail, too. If you are going to team up with a group, I suggest partnering with strangers instead of friends or family. Working with strangers can even create a friendlier, more positive competitive environment not biased by the familial emotion we tend to have and feel for our friends and family if they fail or succeed with us or in spite of us. Either way, choose the group dynamic that will set you up for the highest chance of success.

While I'm not against a shared goal, most people need someone objective to keep them strong-willed and focused on the final outcome. If you and your friends have not demonstrated the resilience needed to stay debt free, then your immediate peer group might not be the best influence. We're human and, therefore, fallible. Teams are only as strong as their weakest link. You might have a great team of friends in mind. I'm not discouraging working in groups. I want to see you succeed whether that means setting a team or individual plan for becoming debt free.

DFDT Key #4: Stick to your plan, unless your plan needs to change.

When it comes to debt management, if you want permanent changes, you have to make permanent lifestyle changes. If you want temporary benefits, by all means make temporary changes, but that will not lead to debt freedom.

I know several services exist now to show your credit score every 2.5 seconds. This constant monitoring of your credit score is pointless and will likely only depress you when you don't see an immediate impact on your score. Once you've implemented a sound plan, let it flow naturally. Checking your credit score every hour on the hour will do nothing but drive you crazy.

I recommend checking your credit score no more than once every one to three months. You only need to monitor your progress to ensure everything is accurate and that no fraudulent charges exist (which is rare). As the debt decreases, it will reinforce what you're doing and make sticking to your plan easier. Again, I won't mislead you into thinking the process will be easy. It will feel very difficult while you're going through it, especially in the beginning, but most things worth having are worth working for.

If you need encouragement, try this simple exercise. Using a free debt calculator, calculate all the money you're wasting right now on debt payments and imagine if all that money was going into your savings account, checking account, children's college fund or any other goal you would rather achieve instead of lining the pockets of your debt collectors. If savings and children's college funds don't motivate you, then imagine all the parties you'll make it rain at while popping bottles on 22-inch rims with your 80 gold chains you bought while going ignorant.

Honestly? I don't care what motivates you as long as you're motivated. Remember, paying off debt is a temporary sacrifice to reach a permanent solution. All you have to do is stick to your plan.

I know it sounds overly optimistic. That's because it is. It's also very possible. You've read my story. It's not like I was the pinnacle of responsibility or beacon of personal discipline. If I can do it, I know you can. I'm not asking you to accomplish anything many others haven't already done for themselves, but this is your life and your debt. You have to make the choice to take the steps to succeed. We all started with no debt. I'm only trying to provide the encouragement you need to return to being debt free. Believe in yourself.

During your journey, you will be your greatest ally. You will also be your own worst enemy. It is through your own determination that you will be debt free or die trying. You can do it. You will do it. I hope this book is one of the many successful steps you've chosen to take towards being debt free.

Lastly, let's review some specific debt payment strategies I used to become debt free.

Debt Free or Die Trying: Payment Strategies

I'm sure there are thousands of different ways to pay off your debt. I used four. For the purpose of this book, I'll cover the four methods I used in chronological order. However, I'll also quantify the difficulty (easy to hard) of each versus their effectiveness (low to high). Unfortunately, the easiest to implement is not the most effective, but I believe they all helped me progress towards my goal so I'll share them all here. As you might expect, I chose the easiest route before finally arriving at the most difficult, yet most effective, choice. You may need to do the same.

I suggest you challenge yourself but you should also use the strategy that will allow you to succeed. Remember, adjust the plan, not the goal.

DFDT Payment Strategy #1: Pay off debt with "whatever is left"

(Quick note, if you're as habitually irresponsible as me, there's rarely anything left).

Ease of Implementation: Easy

Effectiveness of Paying off Your Debt: Low

Strategy: As the name implies, this strategy involves simply taking whatever meager or major sum of money you have left before your next paycheck and applying it towards your preferred debt(s). I say preferred debt, because this "strategy" is the least strategic. It's a starting point.

Example 1: "Whatever is Left"

Description	Amount
Debt	$10,000
Interest Rate	15%
Minimum Payment	$200*
Extra Payment	$0
Total Interest	$15,851
Total Debt + Interest	$25,851
Estimated Payoff	**35 years, 4 months**

Asterisk (*): Each example payment strategy will assume a minimum payment of 2% of outstanding debt. In reality, your lenders may charge more or less.

There are several reasons why this strategy is ineffective. For one, if you're already in debt, you probably don't have much disposable income between paychecks aka you're literally living paycheck-to-paycheck. High interest rates on the credit cards or loans you might have only serve to worsen this issue. Even if you have low-interest rates, you likely have high balances. In a worst-case scenario, you have both high-interest rates and high balances. Therefore, this strategy is the equivalent of throwing a stone in the ocean. While it might create ripples, there is minimal effect on your total ocean of debt.

I only began using this strategy because I was doing nothing to pay off my debts, and I wondered what would happen if I did something crazy, like pay more than the minimum payment some months. This first foray into paying off my debts gave me a taste of what it was like to actually see my balance go down versus up each month. Still, there were far more moral victories than actual victories. The only real benefit to this strategy is that if you keep at it long enough, you might be able to free up enough money to begin moving towards more effective debt payment strategies, like the ones described below.

DFDT Payment Strategy #2: Pay the minimum balance plus a set dollar amount.

Ease of Implementation: Easy

Effectiveness of Paying off Your Debt: Low

Strategy: Similar to Strategy #1, this strategy doesn't take much more work, since most of the math is done for you. You simply take the minimum balance required on each of your cards/loans and pay more. You can do this one of two ways. First, you can choose one card or loan to focus on, which is what I would recommend. Second, you can tackle all of your open cards/loans if you have the available means. Just remember the goal is to start driving down one or all of your balances by paying a set payment that is larger than the minimum balance due each month.

DEBT FREE OR DIE TRYING

Example 2: Minimum Balance + Set Payment

Description	Amount
Debt	$10,000
Interest Rate	15%
Minimum Payment	$200
Extra Payment	$25*
Total Interest	$4,688
Total Debt + Interest	$14,688
Estimated Payoff	**5 years, 6 months**

Asterisk (*): Assumes you pay this fixed amount or more every month until debt free.

While Strategy #2 is more effective than Strategy #1, the main issue is you haven't defined a timeline for your end goal. In addition, how large or small of an amount over the minimum payment you make will be driven by the amount of money you *feel* like paying each month. Put simply, if you

66

pay more, you'll pay your debt off quicker. If you pay less, it will take longer.

This strategy is limited by how effective you decide to make it. If you're like me, it will likely be minimally effective because you'll probably waver from month-to-month or even day-to-day on how much money you feel like paying. Since feelings are rarely as consistent as logic, this strategy tends to vary in effectiveness right along with how responsible you feel like being when your bills are due. This is why as soon as you can do so, you should begin moving towards payment strategy #3 or #4.

DFDT Payment Strategy #3: Pay a randomly set dollar amount.

Ease of Implementation: Moderate

Effectiveness of Paying off Your Debt: Moderate

Strategy: If you make it this far in your debt management journey, or if you're one of those Advanced Placement student types, and you skipped to this step, you'll finally start making a real difference in paying off your debt. I rank this strategy as "moderate" because its success depends completely on you. It could easily be considered highly effective—minus one key component that I'll cover in Strategy #4 in more detail—if you decide to make substantive payments each month.

DEBT FREE OR DIE TRYING

Example 3: Minimum Balance + Randomly Set Payment

Description	Amount
Debt	$10,000
Interest Rate	15%
Minimum Payment	$200
Extra Payment	$50*
Total Interest	$3,950
Total Debt + Interest	$13,950
Estimated Payoff	**4 years, 8 months**

Asterisk (*): Assumes you pay this fixed amount every month until debt free.

The goal with this strategy is to decide on a fixed amount of money you can live without or afford to part ways with each bill cycle. I say "bill cycle", but using your bill's due date isn't the most effective method to use. Although you could easily wait for each bill cycle due date, I have found it's always easier to part with money as soon as possible rather than waiting for a bill collector or bill's due date to demand it from you.

For example, if you get paid on the 1st but your bill isn't due until the 31st, that is 30 whole days when you'll have to be responsible enough to spend your money on the bill rather than, well, anything else more fun than paying bills. You would need exceptional resolve. Let's be honest with ourselves. You're already in debt. If history has been any indication, do you really believe you have the personal resolve to hold on to money any longer than 24-hours, let alone 30, 24-hour consecutive days?

Rather than waiting until the bill is due, I recommend you make a payment as soon as you have the money. If you have $1 dollar more than you need for essentials, then apply that $1 dollar immediately to your debt. If you have $10,000 extra (I'm impressed), pay $10,000 immediately. Trust me. It will always be more difficult to spend money you don't have access to anymore than it will be to wait until that bill's due date.

Right now you may be asking, "How much money should I spend each month?" There's no easy answer to that question. The answer is "there is no wrong answer." You're striving for progress, not perfection. However, one of the easier ways to determine how much money you should allocate towards debt is to use a debt payment calculator of your choice.

This is also why it's important to have a budget. If you don't have a budget, there's no time like the present to develop one. I don't have a specific recommendation for a budget or debt payment calculator but plenty of apps exist to help. Excel works just fine, as does a regular 10-key calculator, a pencil and a piece of paper.

Don't make creating your budget complicated. You only need an estimated budget to establish a framework for this specific strategy. It doesn't have to be exact. Of course the more accurate your budget the more helpful it will be to you, but don't become paralyzed by unneeded analysis if your income changes as frequently as the wind blows. Even an informed guesstimate is better than having no budget at all.

All you need to come up with a rough debt payment estimate is how much money you make each month on average (total income), how much money you owe others (total bills), and how much you commit to miscellaneous expenses, including entertainment and fun (discretionary expenses). Your estimate should look something like this:

Total Income –Total Bills – Discretionary Expenses =

Discretionary Income (Your Budget)

See, nothing fancy. But, now that you know your "Discretionary Income" you can do one of two things. First, you can allocate 100% of your discretionary income to your debt payment plan (which is what I would recommend). However, if you're like me, you probably don't want to. If you're just getting started on paying off your debts, this strategy is also extremely difficult to implement because you're basically going from 0 to 100 real quick. Choosing to part with money you don't have to part ways with is difficult. Procrastination is a hell of a drug.

DEBT FREE OR DIE TRYING

You should pay as much toward your debt as you're comfortable giving away each month. Remember, you're not giving it away in vain. You're paying other people, but in the long run you're paying yourself because one day, done correctly, you will be completely debt free. A little (or a lot, depending on your threshold) of pain now will lead to a world of freedom in the future. If you can willingly part with all of your discretionary income, you'll be far better served and closer to your goals of debt freedom. Ultimately, do what works for you, especially in the beginning. Like a fitness routine, you can always turn up the difficulty level as you get in better shape coping mentally with the idea of having less discretionary income.

Strategy #4 is by no coincidence the most difficult and most effective strategy, which is why it took me so long to reach this inevitable, yet obvious, conclusion on my journey to debt freedom. In its simplest form, this strategy is just another variation of all of the above strategies with a focus on all their best attributes. It also factors in the most critical variable: TIME.

DFDT Payment Strategy #4: Pay a fixed dollar amount based on a fixed debt payoff timeline.

Ease of Implementation: Hard

Effectiveness of Paying off Your Debt: High

Strategy: You'll notice that unlike most debt payment books, nowhere in this book do I cover a roll-up, roll-down or roll-anywhere strategy. That's because I think none of those things really matter. There will always be better, faster, or

71

quicker methods of accomplishing your goals, but none of them will matter if you constantly fall off and start over.

What I have found is the most important strategy for debt freedom success is to pick a plan (or plans) that you can actually stick to. It really doesn't matter if you follow this book or another other book, blog, article or tip from a friend, stranger or expert. If it works for you, follow it. The plan that works for you and is tailored to your goals will, in my opinion, always be the most effective plan.

The key difference between strategy #4 and the other strategies I've outlined is time. There's a saying that a goal without a timeline is a fantasy. I try not to be that pessimistic, but when it comes to debt management, the truth of that statement is inescapable. The beautiful thing about time is it waits for no one. Adding something as simple as a time-specific goal to your plan forces you to succeed or fail— although I would more reasonably view it as an opportunity to redefine your goal than to view it as a failure. Let me show you why time is so critical for the success of any debt payment strategy.

DEBT FREE OR DIE TRYING

Example 4: Minimum Balance + Fixed Payment

Description	Amount
Debt	$10,000
Interest Rate	15%
Minimum Payment	$200
Extra Payment	$200*
Total Interest	$2,065
Total Debt + Interest	$12,065
Estimated Payoff	**2 years, 6 months**

Asterisks (*): Estimated example of a fixed payment (increase or decrease to adjust for your available discretionary income).

Time: In the four "$10,000 in debt" examples above, paying $200 over the minimum payment saves you over 33 years and almost $14,000 in interest payments.

Once again, there are plenty of apps and debt payment calculators available. I'm not partial to any of them, because they all help you accomplish the same purpose: define when you want to pay off your debt and exactly how much money you need to pay each month to achieve your goal.

The mistake most people make when tackling debt, present company included, is we never accurately calculate how long it will take us to do so. With an infinite timeline, most people will give up, fall off and/or fail completely. I cannot emphasize enough how important defining exactly when you want to be out of debt will be for helping you reach your goal. It might take one year or ten years but at least now you actually know. In my opinion, time is the most important factor in setting a reasonable debt payment strategy.

Once you've chosen a timeframe and exact amount of debt you'll need to pay each month, all you have to do is simultaneously the easiest and most difficult part: stick to the plan. It really is that simple, and that difficult. Assuming you don't run into any major hardships, changes in APR rates or increase your debt while attempting to pay off your debt, you will succeed. It's impossible not to.

Finally, please remember that you can change the plan, but never change your goal: debt free or die trying.

About the Author

Originally born and raised in the great state of Texas, Marcus obtained a bachelor's degree in business after surviving the mean streets of the inner suburbs. Since that time, some of the nicer names he has been called include freelance writer, blogger, author, auditor and most relevant to this book, "debt free".

There are myriad details to his upbringing, but most importantly, Marcus was born in the Millennial generation start-up year of 1982. According to questionably reliable data, yet repeatedly published in the news so it must be true, Millennials – and therefore Mr. Garrett – is predisposed to: use sarcasm as a self-coping mechanism, have average education yet grandiose self-esteem buoyed by unchecked ego inflation and years of unearned participation trophies and likely makes up for what he lacks in focus with misplaced discipline. The exhaustive shortcomings of his fellow generational aristocrats are further amplified by a sense of entitlement, apathy, narcissism and a need for constant praise and affection. Tragically, these many faults do not even include the untold but undoubtedly negative effects of rap music and the internet.

Mr. Garrett is too indifferent to correct what might very well be misplaced assumptions about himself and his peers. Therefore, he spends most days humbly expanding upon his vast collection of participation trophies while meandering through life unencumbered neither by debt, burden or worry for anything that extends beyond the length of his nose. When Marcus is not working, he is usually found on various social media platforms offering a plethora of unsolicited opinions.

A decade of audit experience in fields as diverse as criminal justice, law enforcement and health care combined with freelance writing on topics ranging from current events to love and relationships helped him develop a uniquely qualitative and quantitative writing style. The Debt Free or Die Trying book keeps readers entertained with a combination of cautionary scared-straight tales and helpful tips for staying out of debt getting out of debt or. Marcus is very passionate about serving others and looks forward to identifying more ways to support people who can relate to his story with managing, reducing and paying off their debt through continued efforts at DebtFreeorDieTrying.com.